Sometimes I Drive My Mom Crazy, But I Know She's Crazy About Me

by Lawrence E. Shapiro, Ph.D.
Illustrated by Timothy Parrotte
Self-Esteem Series Editor: Hennie M. Shore

Published by:
The Center for Applied Psychology, Inc.
P. O. Box 1587
King of Prussia, PA 19406 U.S.A.
Tel. 1-800-962-1141

The Center for Applied Psychology, Inc. is publisher of Childswork/Childsplay, a catalogue of products for mental health professionals, teachers and parents who wish to help children with their social and emotional growth needs.

Copyright ©1993 by The Center for Applied Psychology, Inc.
Printed in the United States of America

ISBN 1-882732-03-0

Other products by The Center for Applied Psychology, Inc.

Play-and-Read Series Books
ALL ABOUT DIVORCE
TAKE A DEEP BREATH: The Kids' Play-Away Stress Book

Psychological Games
KIDS' DAY IN COURT
MY TWO HOMES
NEVER SAY NEVER
STOP, RELAX & THINK
THE ANGRY MONSTER MACHINE
THE CLASSROOM BEHAVIOR GAME
THE DINOSAUR'S JOURNEY TO HIGH SELF-ESTEEM
THE GOOD BEHAVIOR GAME
THE GREAT FEELINGS CHASE
YOU & ME: A GAME OF SOCIAL SKILLS

For a free catalogue of books, games and toys to help children, call 1-800-962-1141.

Sometimes I Drive My Mom Crazy, But I Know She's Crazy About Me

A Self-Esteem Book for ADHD Children

by Lawrence E. Shapiro, Ph.D.

Illustrated by Timothy Parrotte

◆

The Center for Applied Psychology, Inc.
King of Prussia, Pennsylvania

I have ADHD.* That's what they call some kids who are pretty smart, and sometimes really smart, but have trouble paying attention and sometimes act wild and crazy.

*ADHD stands for Attention Deficit Hyperactivity Disorder. It is a common diagnosis affecting an estimated three to five percent of school-aged children. It is defined by very specific criteria and the correct diagnosis must be made by a qualified professional.

When you have ADHD, you can get into a lot of trouble. I used to get hassled all the time at school, and at home, too. It seemed like everyone was always bugging me about my behavior.

My mom used to call me a "little tornado." She said I drove her crazy.

But now I know how to act the way she wants me to.

My teacher, Mrs. Cooper, used to say, "Can't you *ever* sit still for one single second?" She acted *so dumb*.

But now I pay attention and listen (most of the time), and when I want to ask a question I raise my hand (most of the time).

I used to feel different from all the other kids. I used to feel weird. I got punished and blamed for things that weren't my fault (sometimes). I hated going to school.

Sometimes I felt stupid. But I learned that everyone is good at some things and not so good at others.

My dad says that's a really good attitude to have.

When you have ADHD, sometimes you get too excited about things.

Like sometimes I would get really wild when I was out shopping with my family.

I'd run around the mall.
I'd grab stuff off the grocery shelves.
And once at a drug store I even put something in my pocket.

But my dad saw me and made me put it back (I was really mad, but I knew he was right).

Now I know how to calm myself down when I get too excited.

I take a deep breath and count to 10, really slowly.

And I hardly ever get in trouble anymore. If I do, I say "I'm sorry" (and I really am). If I do something wrong, I try to make it right. My mom says that's called "being responsible."

I have a lot of things now that help me—at home and at school (I think some of the other kids are a little jealous).

I got a lot of help from other people to learn how to do all this. And this book is about how it happened.

I used to really, really hate school. I thought it was terrible. It was stupid. I couldn't wait for the 3:20 bell to ring.

Mrs. Cooper yelled at me every day—at least once, usually more.

She'd say,
"I'm moving your desk to the front of the room."
Or,
"Go to the principal's office and tell him what you just did."
Or,
"Well, we'll just have to call your parents about this, won't we?"

Mrs. Cooper would make me stay inside during recess almost every day.

She'd make me write "I WILL LEARN TO PAY ATTENTION" a zillion times on the blackboard. Lots of times I thought my arm would fall off. Then she'd make me erase the whole board.

But now Mrs. Cooper and I get along just fine. She smiles at me and pats me on the head (yuck!) and we have a lot of special "deals."

Things started to get better when I went to see a lady at my school named Mrs. Greene. My mom said she was a psychologist. That's a person who you can talk to when stuff bothers you.

Mrs. Greene used to see me in her office on Tuesdays at 2 o'clock. She gave me some tests and played some games with me and we talked and she was pretty cool.

Then one day, Mrs. Greene met with my mom and my dad and Mrs. Cooper and the principal and some other people too, in the lunchroom.

I thought, "Boy, am I in trouble now!" but when the meeting was over my mom gave me a hug, Mrs. Cooper smiled at me, and Mrs. Greene winked at me (or maybe she got some gook in her eye).

The next day, I think it was Wednesday, Mrs. Greene called me into her office. She said, "Everyone who was at the meeting wants to help you to feel better about school. We know that you are very smart, but that you have some problems controlling yourself."

"We think that what you have is called ADHD. That means 'attention deficit disorder with hyperactivity.' It's a fancy way of saying that some of the chemicals in your brain make you think differently so that you have a hard time paying attention and sometimes do things without thinking them through.

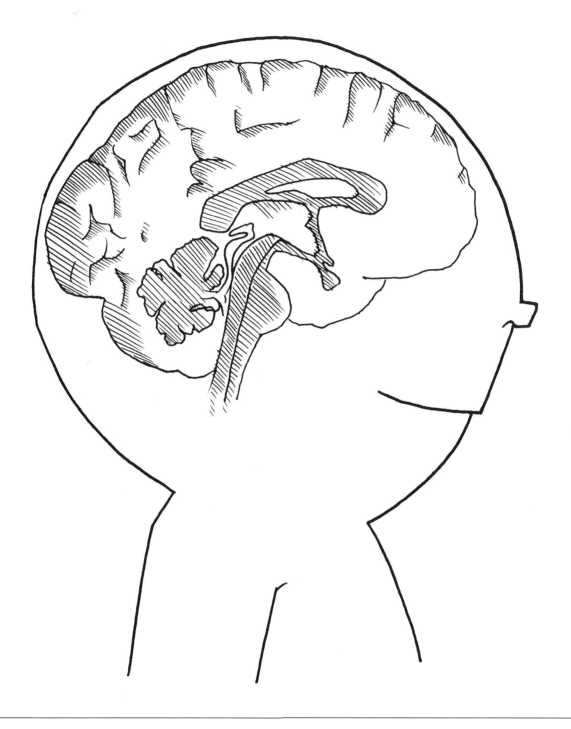

"A lot of children have ADHD. We think that it's something that children inherit from their families, like the color of your eyes or how tall you will be.

"Even though children sometimes see a doctor for ADHD, and sometimes they even take medicine for it, it's not like having chicken pox or a broken arm. When you have the chicken pox you have red spots and a fever. When you have a broken arm it hurts when you move it and you can see the broken bone on an X-ray.

"But the only way you can tell if a kid has ADHD is by the way he acts. Kids with ADHD usually have trouble learning in school and often get into trouble."

Mrs. Greene said that there are lots of ways kids can learn to live with ADHD, but one of the best ways is by using what she called a "behavior chart."

She said, "A behavior chart helps you and the people who work with you to think of certain things that need improvement; things that are important to your teacher and to your parents. Everybody works with you to set goals, and when you do well at these goals, you get stickers on the chart. And when you get 15 stickers you get a special prize."

Mrs. Greene talked to my teacher and they made a chart that looked like this:*

*A blank version of this chart appears on page 125 and may be copied for your use.

But it wasn't that easy. *The first weeks I just got five stickers!*

Mrs. Cooper said, "I know you can try a little harder."

My parents said, "Can't you try a little harder?"

I wanted to say, "Get off my case!" but I didn't. So instead I said, "Yeah, I guess so," and I decided that I *could* try just a *little* harder.

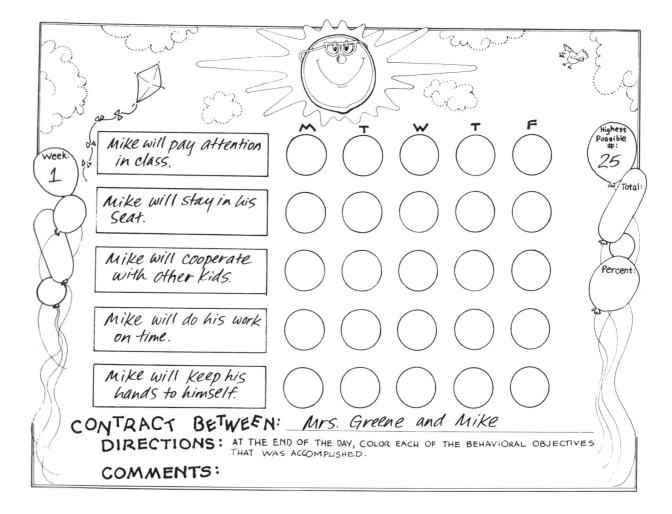

I liked this idea. If I could win 15 stickers I could get a new micro car for my collection.

Mrs. Greene told my parents to be patient, but my mom made a face when she heard that.

Six weeks later I still hadn't gotten the micro car. My mom and dad and I went back to see Mrs. Greene with all my charts. She put them out on a table and then she drew a picture, which she said would help us figure out what the real problem was.

She said it was a "giraffe," but it didn't look anything like a giraffe—it looked like the way I draw mountains. Everyone thought it was really funny that I thought she said "giraffe." That's when I realized she had said "graph."

This is what the graph looked like (I still think it looks like the way I draw mountains):

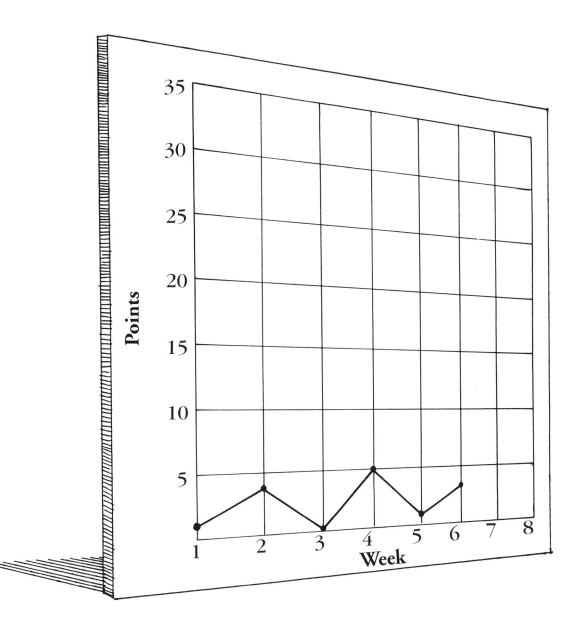

Mrs. Greene said that she wanted me to talk to a special doctor, Dr. Allendale, who might have some other ideas to help me control myself better—and help me get my micro car.

She said that Dr. Allendale would give me some tests and that he might want me to take medicine which would help me control my behavior.

She showed me a picture of what my graph should look like. I said it looked more like stairs than mountains.

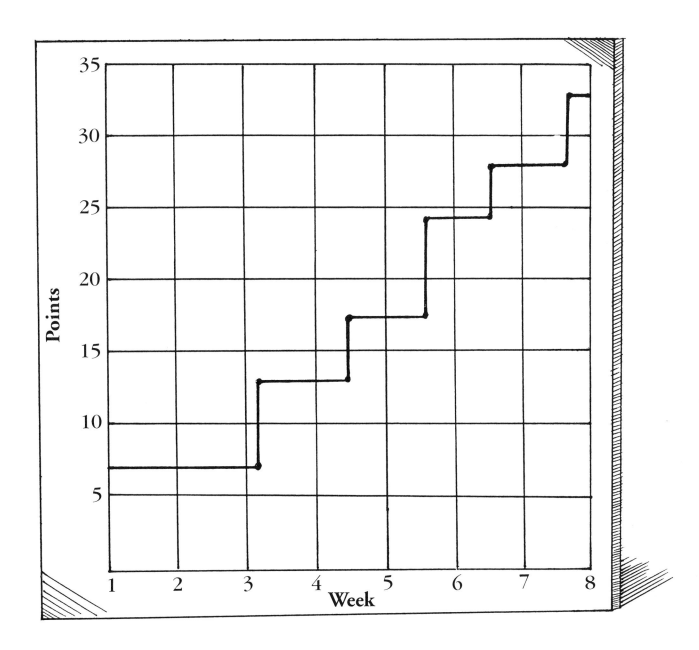

Mrs. Greene said, "They do look like stairs. When you get to the top of the stairs, you'll get your prize and you'll be behaving much, much better."

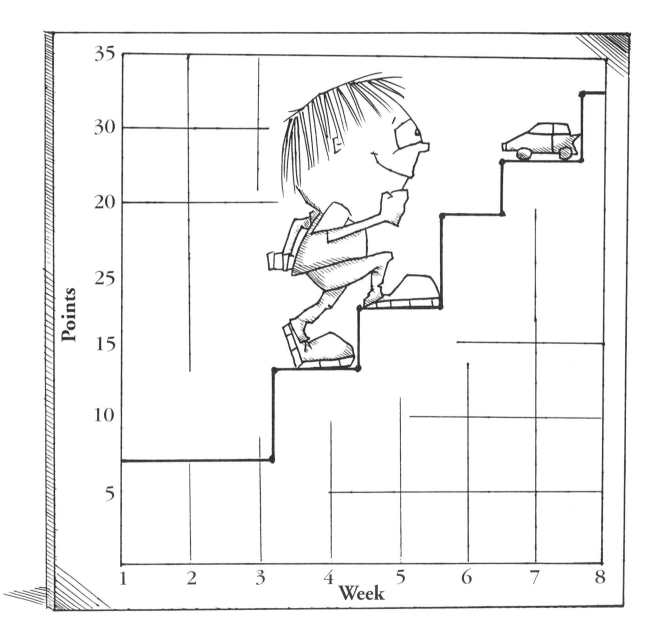

When I went to see Dr. Allendale, he gave me things to draw and puzzles to put together and all sorts of stuff to do. Some were kind of cool and some were kind of stupid.

He also gave me a check-up (Mom called it a "physical examination") like I get right around my birthday—but it was okay because I didn't get any shots!

Then he met with my mom and dad, and then I came in too.

Dr. Allendale said that he thought that I should take a kind of medicine called Ritalin®,* which he said would help me control myself better and get my prize.

*Ritalin® is the brand name for methylphenidate, by far the most common chemical substance used for medication intervention for ADHD. Like any medication, there may be side effects and contraindications to methylphenidate. If this, or any other medication is prescribed for children, its effects must be monitored and supervised closely.

Dad didn't look too happy, but Dr. Allendale said, "We'll just try this for a while and if it doesn't work then we'll stop it right away."

Dr. Allendale said, "I'll check with you every day, at first, to see if the medicine is working," and Dad said, "Okay."

Mom told me that Ritalin® helps lots of kids who have problems with ADHD. She said that there was no way of knowing for sure whether or not it would really help until I tried it.

The next time I saw Mrs. Greene we talked about my medication and she told me that everyone agreed that the Ritalin® was helping me (I already knew this because I had seven stickers—and the week wasn't over yet!).

Everything started going better at school, but sometimes I still drove my mom crazy.

One day I was having a really bad day. A glass broke at breakfast (Mom tried to blame that on me) and I got into a fight with my dumb sister. Oh yeah, and I lost my book report that my dad had typed for me.

Mom said, "You are driving me *CRAZY*! I don't know what to do with you sometimes!" and she gave me a look that really scared me.

I said, *"WHY DON'T YOU JUST PUT ME IN THE TRASH CAN AND THROW GARBAGE ON ME?!!!"*

And then she got really mad and said some things that I forget now and made me go to my room for being a "little smart-you-know-what."

The next day, my mom went to see Mrs. Greene. Mrs. Greene told her that kids like me can be hard to live with sometimes, but that there are things that *she* could do to help.

She told my mom to organize my room for me. My mom put labels on all my drawers and got me cubbies for my stuff.

PANTS

SHIRTS

PAJAMAS

She told my mom to put a chart listing my chores on the refrigerator and to give me a "plus" every time I did what I was supposed to.

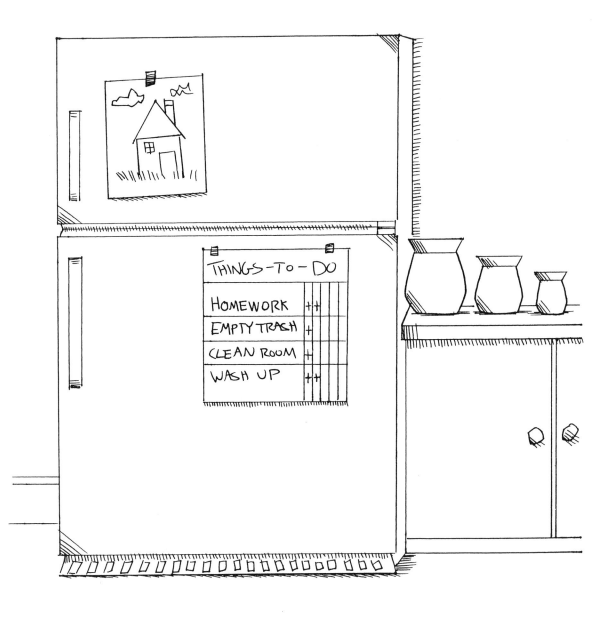

And she told my mom about a group of other moms and dads who also had kids with ADHD and had meetings to discuss stuff about their kids.*

*C.H.A.D.D. (Children with Attention Deficit Disorders) is a national support organization for information on Attention Deficit Disorders. Local chapters hold meetings once or twice a month to discuss issues related to ADD and ADHD. Meetings are attended by parents, professionals and ADD adults. For information about this organization and the chapter nearest you, call or write: C.H.A.D.D., 499 NW 70th Ave., Suite 308, Plantation, FL 33317; (305) 587-3700.

Mom has been going to those meetings, and she really likes them. She goes every month. Whenever she comes home from a meeting she gives me a big hug and kiss (yuck!).

My parents also talk to Mrs. Greene sometimes. She's helping them to learn how to help me, and she's helping them be smarter, too.

Like on weekends, I used to be kind of bored and lonely.

Mom would say, "Call a friend."

But I really didn't have any friends. I'd say, "Nah." And I'd just play my video games.

And then Mom would shake her head and walk away, saying, "Okay, if that's what you want to do."

But last Saturday when I said that, Mom said, "That's enough of video games for today," and she made me call Tommy Johnson from my class at school.

Tommy seemed really glad that I called. He lives next to a playground and we shot baskets and stuff all day and his mom made brownies and he showed me his baseball card collection.

When my mom called, I didn't want to leave. So I stayed and played some more.

And my dad's getting smarter, too.

He knows that I'm not as good as some of the other kids in my class at baseball. I strike out most of the time, and they always put me in right field 'cause they think no one will hit there.

So one day my dad said, "Sometimes it takes a while to find out what you're really good at," and he took me bowling and I found out that *I really am* good at bowling.

We go bowling all the time now and I get strikes and spares. Dad says I'm almost as good as he is!

Mrs. Greene had some good advice to tell my teacher, too. I'm not exactly sure what it means, but I put it in this book in case you want to show your teacher:

Five Things Teachers Can Do To Help A.D.H.D. Kids.

1. A.D.H.D. kids do best when tasks are new and stimulating. They do worst on tasks that are boring or too familiar.

2. A.D.H.D kids do best on tasks where there is frequent feedback.

3. A.D.H.D. kids do best when there is an immediate consequence to their performance (like in Nintendo® games). A token economy, or other behavioral system where points are given and taken away, can be effective in motivating A.D.H.D. children.

4. A.D.H.D kids have difficulty in following rules and self-regulating their behavior. Keep rules simple and clear. Structure time and activities as much as possible.

5. A.D.H.D kids always do best when they get close adult supervision. Make sure that they have adequate supervision with aides or tutors so that they can fulfill their academic potential.

One day I asked Mrs. Greene, "How many kids are there with ADHD?"

She said, "There are millions of children in the United States with some form of ADHD, but it's really hard to tell. Children with ADHD act differently from each other and that's a problem for the people who are trying to help them.

"Kids don't know when they have ADHD, and sometimes grown-ups aren't sure either. There are some tests, like the ones Dr. Allendale gave you, that help them decide if you really have ADHD and if medicine will help you.

"But having a name for the problem really isn't as important as solving the problem. That's why you work on behavior charts at home and at school and that's why you take medicine. When you get more points on your chart, like you did this week, we know that you are getting better.

"It's also very important that you learn in school. Your teacher tells me that you are better at listening in class and that you're turning in your homework every day!"

Then Mrs. Greene said something really cool.

"You know," she said, "there are a lot of grown-ups who have had ADHD or other kinds of learning problems, but they learned to understand that they were a little different and they still did well in school.

"I know this first-hand, because when my husband was your age, he acted just like you! Now he's a lawyer, and a father too, and he does a lot in our community.

"But when he was your age he was very wild. He had trouble all through school. His mom kept every one of his report cards and gave them to him when he was older. You should see what his teachers said about him!"

That was when she reached into her desk drawer and took out one of her husband's report cards to show me. When she handed it to me she said, "When you look at it, remember, my husband went on to college and law school and did really well."

Here's what the report card looked like:

REPORT CARD

SUBJECT	GRADE	COMMENTS
History	F	"Robert is a very difficult child. I hope he improves with time."
English	D	"This is Robert's best grade for the year! Can't he do better?"
Physical Education	B	"Robert runs very well, but I wish he could pay more attention to the rules."
Mathematics	F	"Robert needs a great deal of help in this subject."
Art	F	"Robert never pays attention and cannot sit still. Please talk to him about this!"

Mrs. Greene also told me about a bunch of famous people who had trouble in school, like Magic Johnson and Tom Cruise and really smart people like Thomas Edison.

If you have ADHD, I hope my book has helped you feel better about it.

I know that I feel a lot better than I used to, because I was able to get help from the people who really care about me. The charts and stickers really helped, and so did the medicine. Stuff like finding out that I'm good at bowling and that I can have a lot of fun with Tommy made me feel pretty good too. And I finally did get my micro car!

I know one thing—I could never have changed this much before I got help.

I still drive my mom crazy sometimes. But I know she's crazy about me!

Epilogue

Attention Deficit Hyperactivity Disorder (ADHD) is one of the most common diagnoses of school-age children, and, at the same time, it is one of the most problematic to treat. ADHD children are typically perceived as "difficult" children, both at home and at school, and they know it. Their sense of themselves as "rejected" by adults and/or "inferior" to other children may be more of a problem than the ADHD itself.

Self-esteem is more than just liking oneself. It is a deep and overriding sense of self-worth and well-being, which comes from a realistic sense of competency and success in the world. But how can this be achieved with children who are characterized as "problem" children?

It is difficult to say whether using the term "ADHD" *with* children will help or hinder them in developing a positive self-image. First, we must make sure that this is an accurate diagnosis. The diagnosis of Attention Deficit Disorder, with or without Hyperactivity, can only be made by a qualified professional. Then we must weigh the benefits vs. the detriments of telling a child that he has ADHD.

Perhaps the most important benefit of acknowledging the "label" is that this diagnosis has recently been recognized by federal education guidelines as qualifying a child for the spectrum of special education services. Secondly, we must consider the need to be truthful with a child. If the adults in a child's world are using this term frequently and thinking of the child as an "ADHD child," then the child will pick up on this, whether or not ADHD is discussed directly with him. Finally, we must consider the benefit for the child of understanding his own problem. Most professionals agree that it is important for children to understand their strengths and weaknesses in order to set realistic goals.

There are, however, contraindications to telling a child that he has ADHD. Some children react very negatively to the notion that they are "different." Others may use this as an "excuse" to make less than a full effort at school or at home. Each child with ADD or ADHD must be considered as unique, and, if appropriate, professional advice should be sought as to how much or how little to tell a child about ADHD.

This book tells the story of one boy who has developed a sense of self-worth by learning to deal with his problems as he is encouraged by the help of the adults around him. ADHD children have complex problems and solutions are equally complex. But the interventions in this book are the ones supported by years of research. They include: behavioral programs at home and in school; educational management; parent support groups; finding appropriate role models; attention to the social development of these children; and, in many cases, medication.

The main purpose of this book is to help children and adults see these interventions as realistic and appropriate approaches, and to develop a positive sense of self-esteem based around their efforts. We know from years of research that ADHD is a problem that changes as a child grows older, but doesn't go away. It is important for children to develop appropriate coping mechanisms that will help them function at their highest level at any age.

In addition to the programs and approaches discussed in this book adults who work with ADHD children should follow the following principles:

- Seek positive opportunities for children to excel.
- Give children a realistic view of their world.
- Give children the opportunity to learn their strengths and weaknesses and to develop themselves.
- As adults, you must show children, by example, the importance of having a positive attitude.
- Learn all you can. There is a great deal of information and many resources to help ADHD children, their parents, and their teachers.

While there are no easy or direct paths to take in working with ADHD children, it is our hope that this book provides some road signs on your important journey.

Using Behavior Charts

Behavioral programs have been proven to be among the most effective methods for helping children with a variety of problems. Forms are an integral part of every behavioral program, giving immediate feedback to the child, charting progress, and motivating the child to succeed. Remember that behavioral programs rely on very specific principles, which must be respected in the design and implementation of the program. Factors to consider include:

1. Set realistic goals and objectives which are observable and measurable.
2. Provide appropriate motivation for change.
3. Provide feedback at intervals appropriate to the child's age and resistance of the child to change.
4. Plan for long-term as well as short-term change.
5. Consider other factors which may be reinforcing old behaviors or interfering with change.
6. Plan for a phasing-out of the program and generalization of the behavioral change.
7. Be positive and consistent in implementing the program.

Following are three charts/graphs for use with ADHD children, including a behavior chart for charting five individual behaviors (pg. 125), a monthly graph to plot points earned over a month's period (pg. 126), and "a good and bad" behavior chart that can be used to chart a wide variety of behaviors (pg. 127).

Highest Possible #:

Total:

Percent:

F

T

W

T

M

CONTRACT BETWEEN: _____

DIRECTIONS: AT THE END OF THE DAY, COLOR EACH OF THE BEHAVIORAL OBJECTIVES THAT WAS ACCOMPLISHED.

COMMENTS:

Week:

GOOD & BAD BEHAVIORS

NAME _____

WEEK OF _____

DAY _____

"+" GOOD

____ PAYS ATTENTION
____ RAISES HAND
____ LISTENS WELL
____ ASKS FOR HELP
____ WAITS HIS/HER TURN
____ WORKS HARD
____ IS POLITE
____ HAS A POSITIVE ATTITUDE
____ FOLLOWS RULES
____ KEEPS HANDS TO HIS/HERSELF
____ HELPS FELLOW CLASSMATES
____ HELPS TEACHER
____ WORKS WELL WITH CLASSMATES
____ FINISHES ASSIGNMENTS ON TIME
____ CONTROLS HIS/HER BEHAVIOR

OTHER:
____ ____
____ ____
____ ____

____ TOTAL

"–" BAD

____ HITS CLASSMATES
____ TEASES CLASSMATES
____ TALKS OUT LOUD IN CLASS
____ DOESN'T COMPLETE HOMEWORK
____ BREAKS RULES
____ DOES NOT LISTEN WELL
____ STEALS
____ LIES
____ COPIES NEIGHBOR'S PAPER
____ BULLIES OTHERS
____ IS A TATTLE-TALE
____ DOESN'T PAY ATTENTION
____ DOESN'T STAY IN LINE
____ HAS A NEGATIVE ATTITUDE
____ IS IMPOLITE

OTHER:
____ ____
____ ____
____ ____

____ TOTAL

____ DAILY TOTAL (SUBTRACT "–" FROM "+")

Resources

Books

Bain, L. (1991). *A Parent's Guide to Attention Deficit Disorders.* New York: Bantam Doubleday Dell.

Barkley, R. (1991). *Attention-Deficit Hyperactivity Disorder: A Clinical Workbook.* New York: Guilford Press.

Barkley, R. (1990). *Attention Deficit Hyperactivity Disorder: A Handbook for Diagnosis and Treatment.* New York: Guilford Press.

Gardner, R.A. (1987). *Hyperactivity, The So-Called Attention-Deficit Disorder, And The Group of MBD Syndromes.* Cresskill, NJ: Creative Therapeutics.

Gehret, J. (1991). *Eagle Eyes: A Child's Guide to Paying Attention.* Fairport, NY: Verbal Images Press.

Galvin, M. (1988). *Otto Learns About His Medicine: A Story About Medication for Hyperactive Children.* New York: Brunner/Mazel.

Goldstein, S. and Goldstein, M. (1990). *Managing Attention Disorders in Children: A Guide for Practitioners.* New York: John Wiley & Sons, Inc.

Gordon, M. (1991). *ADHD/Hyperactivity: A Consumer's Guide for Parents and Teachers.* DeWitt, NY: GSI Publications.

Ingersoll, B. (1988). *Your Hyperactive Child: A Parent's Guide to Coping with Attention Deficit Disorder.* New York: Bantam Doubleday Dell.

Moss, D. (1989). *Shelley, the Hyperactive Turtle.* Rockville, MD: Woodbine House.

Parker, H. (1992). *The ADD Hyperactivity Handbook for Schools.* Plantation, FL: Impact Publications.

Parker, H. (1988). *The ADD Hyperactivity Workbook for Parents, Teachers and Kids.* Plantation, FL: Impact Publications.

Quinn, P. and Stern, J. (1991). *Putting on the Brakes: Young People's Guide to Understanding Attention Deficit Hyperactivity Disorder (ADHD).* New York: Brunner/Mazel.

Weiss, G. and Hechtman, L. (1986). *Hyperactive Children Grown Up.* New York: Guilford Press.

Videotapes
Goldstein, M. (1991). *It's Just Attention Disorder: A Video Guide for Kids.* Salt Lake City: Neurology, Learning & Behavior Center.

Goldstein, S. (1989). *Why Won't My Child Pay Attention? A Video Guide for Parents of Hyperactive and Inattentive Children.* Salt Lake City: Neurology, Learning & Behavior Center.

Goldstein, S. and Goldstein, M. (1990). *Educating Inattentive Children: A Guide for the Classroom.* Salt Lake City: Neurology, Learning & Behavior Center.

Other Materials
Pay More Attention: A Self-Regulation Program for Children. Impact Publications. Teaches children to self-monitor their on-task behavior utilizing an audiotape which "beeps" at specific intervals.

Stop, Relax & Think. Center for Applied Psychology, Inc. Board game for teaching children ages 6-12 to verbalize their feelings, to practice stopping their motoric action, to relax, and to problem-solve and plan ahead.

All resources listed are available through Childswork/Childsplay, The Center for Applied Psychology, P. O. Box 1587, King of Prussia, PA 19406; toll-free 1-800-962-1141.

About the Author:
Lawrence E. Shapiro, Ph.D. has had more than fifteen years working with children as a teacher, school psychologist, director of a school for special- needs children, and in private practice. He is the author of four books and has invented over a dozen psychological games. Dr. Shapiro is the president of The Center for Applied Psychology, Inc. and the Childswork/Childsplay catalogue, the country's largest distributor of psychologically-oriented toys, games and books.

About the Artist:
Timothy Parrotte was born and raised in Plattsburgh, New York. Trained as a graphic designer at the Art Institute of Philadelphia, he has pursued his greater interest, cartooning and illustration and has made Philadelphia his permanent address.

About the Self-Esteem Series Editor:
A long-time editor and writer for various trade and consumer magazines and periodicals, Hennie M. Shore is now writer/editor for Childswork/Childsplay and The Center for Applied Psychology, Inc. of King of Prussia, Pennsylvania. She resides in Wynnewood, Pennsylvania with her husband and two children.